S0-FBN-913

VILLAGE STREETS

MARY ANN MCDONNELL

VILLAGE STREETS

MARY ANN MCDONNELL

ZEUGPRESS

© 1991 Mary Ann McDonnell

Printed in the United States of America

First Edition

Zeugpress
W. R. Rodriguez, publisher
1802 Redwood Lane
Madison, Wisconsin 53711

TABLE OF CONTENTS

I

II

*For Eddie
and all of our children,
those born of us
and those who have come happily
into our lives,
and for their children.*

I

Village Streets

These are the streets we walked along
A long time ago.
I walk them now alone.
I look in shop windows we looked in then—
"Old George's antiques."

I see he sold a few pieces.
Ah, but the Chinese console table
With the patina of dust
Is still just as it always was.

I can still see your face so clearly darling—

I don't think I'll ever walk down this street again.

Like George's Chinese table
I find
Some memories are best left, undisturbed,
Covered gently with dust.

Some Things Old Men Do, Day In And Day Out

Very early in the morning
They rise
Tread familiar steps
To the bathroom
Perform their ablutions
Then
Put on the coffee pot
Spread generic jam
On generic bread
Reread last night's newspapers
Talk to the bird
Feed the cat
Take the dog out
Exchange a few words
With their young neighbors hurrying off to work
Then
Back to the house
Water the plants
Some of them (promised their wives they would
The wives who died first
Leaving them alone)
Then
They take out the garbage
Throw the spread across the bed
Take books back to the library
The laundry can wait till tomorrow

Old men are busy, busy, busy
Attending to all the tasks
That hurry their days
Till the ten p.m. news
Then they can wind the clock
And tomorrow they must
Take the laundry

Longing

The days go by all quiet.
Sabbath to Sabbath
Another week—
Yet—
Constantly I seek
To hear a word
If only a whisper
From one who could not speak.

Silence, soft as China silk
Fills every room
Of the apartment with nothingness.
Silence trapped—
Holding its breath,
Waiting—
Waiting for the sound of two heart beats.
There is only the beat of one
And
The faithful old clock on the bureau.
These sounds don't count!
He isn't here—

Lonely Room

Sh!
Listen to the falling rain.
Loneliness is here,
Loneliness lives in the shadows of this room—
My lamp gives little comfort,
The rain keeps falling,
My tears are falling too—
My heart asks *where are you*?

Hospital Night

Doors open and close, open, close.
People come and go.
Life centimeters along in unquiet rooms.
It rides gurneys
Up and down hallways through the night—
Some nights are so noisy—

Suddenly a sharp stab of pain.
Astonished I hear myself cry out.
I ask for help—
Exposing a frightened, naked heart—

A nurse comes, she is talking to me,
I know she is, I can see her lips moving.
Why can't I hear her?
She raises my bed then leaves the room.
Sweat is pouring baptismally from my head.
Salt burns my eyes, flavors my lips.

The nurse has come back; she hands me a plastic cup.
I can hear her now, she says words
Like codeine, morphine—
    words that have become my bread and water
My life—

When morning comes I am getting out of here!

Too much death—
Too much life—

Ether

Down, down
Deep
Deeper
Into
That gyroscopic world
Of
Anesthesia
Numbing the pain
Making frenzied the brain, that cavorts
Madly in dayglo colors
Racing wildly
From star to star.

When Visiting Hours Are Over

Dear old man,
Lying there in your metal crib,
An aura of fluorescent light
    always shining down on you.
You ask us, "Is it day or night?"
We tell you it is nighttime,
But you don't really care.
We must be quiet—
You doze off—
But! we don't want to be quiet, we
Want to lift you in our arms, and
Tell you out loud how much we love you,

Tell you that it takes all our strength
To leave you here in this hi-tech
Medieval place, knowing you
Might slip away—and we won't be with you.

What do they do to you
When we go?

We pray they give you a needle of kindness
To free you from the pain for a little while.

Visiting hours are over!

There they've told us again,
We must go now—keep sleeping darling—
We go down in the elevator, dragging your
I.V. pole, your kangaroo bag, your monitor
And all the bleeping machines
With us.
They stay in our minds; we take
Them home with us.
We'll bring them back first thing
In the morning.

Good night, dear heart—

Votive Light

Low soft glow—
Candle in the chapel
Flickering,
Making little piffle noises,
Dying
Going out
Leaving only
Tiny waxen tears
In
A
Little red cup.

"I Am Very Tired Lord"

I got to weeping today
I missed all those who left me—
Family and friends who went away.
They promised we could meet again,
Of course I know they couldn't tell me when—

I should go now Lord—
Really I should—
No one would miss me,
Except maybe old Tabby here—he loves me.
He is old and all alone too.

My head and hands are shaking quite a lot lately.
Please let me go now, Lord take me!
There will be no wake, no Kaddish, no one to notify—

Oh, I am so very tired Lord,
Give me a quiet grave for sleeping,
Then let me waken in your keeping—

The Day After The Funeral

The day slipped—by—by strength of will
Willing the minutes into hours.
Hurry, hurry, hurry into night.
One day less—
Time heals—
Night—be blind, give sleep, give dreams,
Hurry me into that time that heals.

Give me sleep and a dream
That I may journey back again
    If only now and then.

New Widow I

Out of the shadows of this night,
I will rise at dawn
And wonder—
How the sun
Has come again
Now that in all this world
        There is no you.

New Widow II

When the night has died
And the dreams have fled
And you waken again to a half empty bed
You call his name
But
There is no answer.

You lie quite still—until
You remember he is sleeping yet
The other sleep—
So you get up and start your day.
Widows have found
It's always been this way.

"The Pause That Refreshes"

When in body, mind and soul
I grow weary and sore distressed
To renew myself
I send my mind awondering
And—from the coiling, resting roots of faith
Branches spring anew!
I am refreshed,
For answers come to me—
To wonder and to still accept in faith
Is faith as it is meant to be—
Holy mystery.

Forsaking All Others

Some marriages get better and better,
The newness becomes a familiar
    yet everchanging pattern.
There are the ups and downs and the plateaus.
You live and grow and experience all
    the stages of life together—
That's the wonder of it all.
After years, decades,
You reach a zenith where old and new
    and everything along the way
Become the norm.
One day the play ends.
Death who was always in the wings
Enters center stage.
On cue one of you
Must exit.
One is left—
Then one day both of you will
Be opening again, some time, somewhere far,
    far out of town.

Who Is That Knocking On My Door?

Just this morning there came a knocking on my door.
It was a most insistent knocking
    I had never heard before—
I called out rather timidly, "Who is it?"

A voice called back to me,
"It's Old Age"—
Quickly!—
I turned the key and slid the bolt,
And said,
"Go away, the lady that lives here isn't at home"—

Then the voice of Old Age answered,
"That's quite all right,
My dear—I'll wait."

I Remember When Uncle Frank Took Aunt Rose To Live In The City

Don't look in the rear view mirror Rose,
You've seen it all before. The farmhouses with their
Wraparound porches, the trees, the gardens,
What's to look at? Old Joe's tune-up garage
And gas pumps? The corner saloon, the
Cannon and flagpole on the green?
No, Rose, you've seen it all—
Don't look back, Rose, look ahead, look
At it this way—you won't have the big
Old house to keep up now, no more
Gracing things and mowing the lawn, it was
Enough to break your back.
You can get out more, visit the museums,
Take in movies and plays. They'll be sidewalks
And you will be able to walk around all
You want, you'll be doing new things
Meeting new people—believe me Rose
you're going to like it—Don't look back
Rose—
But Rose did look back, and cried,
Strong Aunt Rose cried! God, how he hated
It when she cried—she never used to do
That, but just this last month, what
With getting all her things together, and closing the

House down, she cried and cried.
Three months later Rose found her way back
To the hard-to-take-care-of drafty old house
    in the country.
Back to friendly old ghosts and evergreen memories.
The family was very upset with her
But in time they came around.
I wouldn't be a bit surprised if years
Down the road one of them might
Just find what Rose found in
The old place.

Collectors' Items

Why, oh why do I do this?
Heaven knows I must stop!
Seems to me, I am always saving things.

An ornate old mantlepiece clock
That ticked its last tock
Thirty years ago. (One more thing to dust.)

Faded old letters with expired dates and authors,
Four baby shoes—
One for each child, now an adult.
Why do I keep these old things, things obsolete?
Remnants of broken rosaries, prayers long ago as-
cended,
Pretty buttons,
Odd shaped stones,
A brown gardenia,
All these little bits and pieces of my life
Ratpacking down memory street.

Rainy Night

I listen to the rain—
Whimpering, then roaring all night.
Outside my locked door
It beats a wild staccato on the glass windows
With wind powered fists—
Frantically seeking entrance inside this house.
Does the rain wish to come in out of the storm?
Or can this noisy furor
Be the specter of some old sorrow
Seeking quiet for its tomorrow?

Amnesia

I wrote my Paris memoirs of you
Last night. Wine made the adjectives
Flow and the verbs turn blue.
I wrote and I wrote remembering
Everything about you—you—you—
Ah! But, I wrote with mock pen,
In invisible ink on onion skin.
I wrote it all down—
Everything—
I remembered about you, you, you!

I wrote of you at dawn, at sunset,
In the rain and the summer sun—
I told the whole wide world
How beautiful you were when
Moonbeams played across your
Face—
Yes, indeed I wrote all about you,
you, you—
                    and
                    it's
                    driving
                    me
                    mad
I'll be damned if I can remember
                    your
                    name!

Missing You

Gosh, how I miss those mornings,
When we would "coffee cup talk,"
"You tell me your dreams
I tell you mine."

I miss those times we'd become so into
Each others' words and thoughts
We would miss bus stops.

I don't miss bus stops anymore.
I just
Miss you, miss you, miss you—

Cold Night

Brrr! But it's cold tonight.
The moon shines down all golden bright—
The air is clear.
Swift moving clouds
Grace the landscapes of the sky—
And
Here am I
Walking alone—
On a city street.
My heart recalls another night,
When our universe stood still
And
We warmed our little world
Just walking hand in hand
Counting stars—

II

Whitney Museum Special Showing

Inside the Whitney Museum
Caricatured people ride on Red Grooms' subway car.
Soft-sculpture people are sitting or standing
    propped for a simulated subway ride.

Three got off at Fourteenth Street—
The others on the #6 train ride on uptown.
Strangers all of them,
Yet
They seem familiar somehow.
We're sure we've seen them all before.
On second look,
They kind of look a lot like us,
A lot like us—

A Coin

His shabby suit was worn shiny; dirty and tattered, it looked especially bad in the glint of the sun. His poverty was showing. His palsied hand was filthy. With his palm outstretched, in a very low voice he called, "A coin, a coin."

In a loud, brusque voice a comfortably dressed elderly woman said, "Bum!" Scowling a well practiced scowl she hurried past him. She was the embodiment of judge—jury—and quick indictment.

He just stood there when she had gone; he was a living, breathing person much as she was; he too cast a shadow in the sun—proving his existence.

He never called her a name but she called him one.

Slowly he moved off, dragging his soul with him as he trudged on up First Avenue, trying to pick up a coin along the way.

Good Looking Guy (All Of 17 Years Old)

Look at him—
Just look at him, sitting there in his Hathaway shirt—
He's well aware of his great ancestral genes,
Flaunting his store bought threads,
And
His great good looks—

Boy, doesn't he think he looks great!
And boy doesn't he!

Teenager in Ya Ya's give the teenage girls a treat.

Jukebox

Silver and purple box etched in chrome
Making a Second Avenue pub its home
Eating silver coins
But abstaining from all the liquid delights
Crying out sad songs
Covering the noise of fights
Singing through the nights
Liberace, Humperdink and Bach
Wailing country westerns, disco and rock
Entertaining in a haven of escape
Standing there against the wall—
Indifferent witness to it all.

Girl On Saint Mark's Place

See her
See how slowly she walks,
So slow
So tired,
Not yet twenty—so old!
A child, girl child, old woman—
Drying fast, flower in an autumn garden,
Withering, drying into dying,
Here on the street before our eyes.
She was so fragile, so beautiful, so fair—
Now see her there—
Aged by frenzied, rushing, crushing
Life sucking mad hours.
She is dying, right here
            For all the world to see
            Right here on St. Marks place.

Whore

Whore lady, there is no challenge in your eyes.
You are wearing harlequin clothes.
Where have you left your youth?
You are a living haunt—

Have you ever known love?
Is there someone for whom you really care?

You are always in pursuit of
What you do not want—
Get out!
Take a bus ride!
Get out of this town
Before you're out of time—

Go straight ahead—
Take no backward glance!

Wash your face!
Comb your hair!
Take your soul and go somewhere—

The Traveler

I've never thought of myself as a traveler, but I guess you might call me that. I've been to Europe a few times, lived there awhile, graduated from a university in Paris.

Went to the Orient too at the request of the United States Army, came home and toured most of the states, part of a four year research and study group for one of the Five Hundred Corps. But it wasn't till after all these trips that I really traveled—although I've never moved much below the Brooklyn Bridge on the Manhattan side or above Fourteenth Street east or west here in New York City.

I have traveled far, far from family, friends and stability. I travel light, don't even carry a totebag—I'd only lose it, or worse, have to fight for it!

I fly on the wings of Thunderbird or take Night Trains going nowhere over and over again. I travel fast on a liquid express—

Just bummed another quarter that gives me my fare for one more trip on Night Train. Guess I will just stay on till the end of the line for a few more years—or till tomorrow—or maybe just till the bottom of the bottle. Got my fare, got my ticket, got the bottle—who knows, this might be my last trip.

The Games Go On—

Red light green light,
Red Rover, Red Rover, let Jenny come over—
Hide and seek, Angie's it!
Hop scotch, Betty's got three boxes already.
Hangman, ghost—anyone can play—
Pepper salt mustard cider,
    how many people live in China?
Jump rope—double dutch.
Turn around, turn around, blind's man bluff.
Here we go round the mulberry bush,
Johnny on a pony—one—two—three.
Farmer in the dell, the cheese stands alone—
Three blind mice,
The farmer's wife de-tailated those little devils—
Coffee pot, coffee pot, what am I thinking of?

I am thinking of all those games we played
    when we were kids—
The players have scattered and yet—
The children all grown up
Play games still.

The Last Out

She closed the door behind her
And went out into the new day,
Out of his life forever—

He closed the door behind him
And went out into the night,
Out of her life forever.

Mid daytime and nighttime
They each returned, then together
They closed the door behind them.
They went out out of each
                    Others' lives forever.

He walked west, she took a cab.

Sorely In Need Of A Lie

When I saw you last night, like a fool I said,
"Of course nothing has changed."
The only thing that has changed is everything!
Yes I know how I so fiercely don't love you anymore.
Yes I know how you have come to loathe me.
We don't remember birthdays—
There are no anniversaries—
But oh, oh it's such a beautiful night!
Tell me lies—tell me lies.

Hm! I Wonder About You Silly Clown

You there, silly clown in your harlequin suit—
What are you laughing at?
You have the world on a string
You silly old thing,
Dancing around in a sawdust ring.

Actor, mime, mummer,
What are you really thinking?
Are you laughing with us, or at us?

You obnoxious cuss
Riding through towns in a carnival bus.

Are you just passing through,
To leave us a laugh?
Are you hiding a tear on your funny clown face?
Are you really no different than us?
Do you hurt sometimes?
Are there days when you're very, very happy?
Are there days when you feel so blue you could die?
But,
Clowns aren't supposed to cry
So you don't—
I often wonder about you, dear silly clown.

Arts & Crafts Exhibit
P.S. 34, Room 201

A one legged spider in collage clay
A skinny elephant of papier-mache
A purple sun in a blood red sky
A fat lumpy frog with one great green eye
A square shaped robin with a scotch plaid vest
Ah, three painted stones in a wet paper nest
A rice paper mobile taped to the window shade
A pink tissue rose that will never fade
A stocking stuffed hippo in a popstick zoo
Pipe cleaner people all askew
Just standing at angles with nothing to do.

Snow In The 9th Precinct N.Y.C.

Soft white gauge, thin layered badge
Covering gently the bruised hurt earth
Covering old scars
Hiding new wounds.

Ungainly, crooked tree becomes quiet loneliness.
Snow soundlessly covering, covering—
The ghetto becomes Paris.

What If I Went To Ireland

A road somewhere is calling
To the wanderer in me
Take me to the high roads
Lead me to the sea

Let me cross the ocean
My roots are blooming there
Perhaps I'll find another face
That I'd know anywhere

In Castledown Square

The old women, black skirted, woolen sweatered
Cozy round like storybook witches—
Like cawing blackbirds with nodding heads
They meet on the street, across fences or on doorsteps
To exchange daily news bits of their little village.

If news should be scarce
They re-edit old bulletins.
Their grapevine spares no one—
Father Jim, Himself the mayor, the old and the young,
      and of course "That Callahan Girl."
Their own families must lead dull, exemplary lives
      for their names are never spoken of.

After a time their tongues are exhausted—
The old women in their somber black skirts
      and heavy black sweaters
And their now quiet tongues amble on toward
      their homes satisfied with their latest news analy-
ses.

To Wake The Dead

No rumble of thunder
No knock on the door
Will waken Bill Skag from his sleep.
He died in the night—
Gar what a sight!
He was took with a shaking jag.
Word was around in village and town
That Bill was onto the drink again.

Well now, maybe he was,
And maybe he wasn't—
But right now a wee drop would do me no harm.
(Bill would drink to that
If only he could.)

I believe I'll just have a wee nip to keep me self calm
Till Father Jim reads the 23rd Psalm—

The Old County Champ

He sleeps upon a narrow bed
Far out in the countryside,
The sun and the moon above his head.
There was no funeral,
No one cried.

The old gravedigger doffed his cap,
Mumbled a prayer with liquored breath,
Then he covered the old champ
With a blanket of earth.
He left him to sleep in eternal rest,
His bones to dirt, his last fight to death.

Dreammender

Day in, day out, people bring their broken dreams
To the dreammender's shop.
The smithy works quietly
Putting in long hours,
Seldom sleeping—
Keeps right on working
At
Mending, repairing, making whole again
People's broken dreams.
The sign over his shop reads

> "Dreams mended
> Nightmares discarded
> But
> I don't touch daydreams."

Evening Comes To The Backyard
At 1802 Redwood Lane

The last bird has finished chattering.
All the goodnights have been said.
Little fists of feathers
Fill the dormitories in the trees.
The sun goes down,
The moon comes on—a night light—
Casting shadows.
Grass is heavy with dew.
The only sound—
The porch swing moving softly,
Caught in a vagrant night breeze.

Pussywillows Make Me
Feel So Sad

Pussywillows make me feel so sad.
All fat and furry
Full term kittens
Stillborn—
They stay forever
On their mother branch
Never to roam or to play
Or do the things that kittens do,
Never to really come alive.
Stillborn
Little
Puff
Of
Grey
Fluff
You make me feel so sad.

First Frost

The first frost had come in the night and
Not disappearing before noon,
Cleverly disguised itself as white
Chrysanthemums—

Autumn

The leaves bid each other adieux
Their close affinity through the summer is over
Soon they will belong to no season
October rains will leave the trees
Naked, barren, brown
A
Forest
Of
Crucifixes—

Come Fill The Cup

Spring rain had come in the night . . .
Gently,
Filling every cup of tulip up—

The Thief

Pride of ancient Japan,
Pure silk tapestry,
Embroidered with threads of gold
By an artist's hand—
Gift for the emperor,
Stolen by one tiny moth.

No Pets Allowed
(Sign On Front Window Of Abandoned
Tenement)

No pets allowed?
No pets at all?
But there are pets you know—
There are mice in the wall,
Roaches run in the hall.
Spiders make webs to catch green bottle flies,
Dust kittens float everywhere.
There are pigeons on the window sill.
Squirrels run in and out through broken window-
panes.
Mosquitoes at night
Take bloody bites,
And
There are other creeping, crawling things
Entomologists have yet to identify—
No pets allowed?
No pets indeed!
My, my, my—

Forecast

The bushes down near the barn are covered
    with blackbirds—
So many of them, they swarm like bees.
Their black feathers ruffle and shimmer—
They chatter, chirp and caw.
En masse they mimic perpetual motion.
High anxiety!
Suddenly a hush, stillness, a quiet waiting—
Waiting for a cue?
Moma looks at them, then looks skyward.
Moma says, "A storm is coming."
A sudden noisy ruffling of feathers and flapping
wings—
      They lift off—
Swept swiftly up into the sky.
They become a crooked shadow against the sun,
A great black fan—
Poof! they are gone.

Moma is right, thunder rumbles in the distance.

What Do Little Boys Keep In Old Cigar Boxes?

Why treasures of course!
Aggies, glassies, and cat eyes
Cola caps filled with wax for corner-to-corner,
     skelly
Priceless cards of Whitey Ford, Mickey Mantle, Hodges
     and Joltin' Joe DiMaggio.
Yes lots and lots of magical things—
A two-ply weight of good kite string
Assorted fishing weights and flies
Two broken pen knives with Empire State and
     Niagara Falls painted right on them
Some bubble gum hard enough to break a tooth
A rubberband that will never expand
A medal all dull with a ribbon decrepit
Won years ago at the Fourth of July Community Fest
Two ticket stubs to a Yankee game
A rusty jew's harp and a cracked kazoo
Yes sirree—
Little boys keep all their "good stuff"
In old cigar boxes—
I thought you knew . . .

Noise And Violence

Surf pounds the shore—
Lightning crackles—
Thunder crashes—
Winds roar!
There is violence in tornados!
And
Out in the kitchen,
Grandma beats the eggs—and—whips the mashed
    potatoes!
Violence is everywhere—
Do you suppose, perhaps
The earth did start with a big bang?

The Great Debate

The Id and the Ego
Discussed one day
Their relative worth.

Ego said
I am a very fine thing
I stand for reason, for sanity
I make man aware of himself
I make him healthfully conceited
I am that part of his psyche that
Gives him his rationality—
Yes indeed, I am a very fine thing.

Then Id
Spoke up
I am more important
I am a much finer thing
I am that part of the psyche which is
The very source of all energy—
Indeed I am a very fine thing.
Remember that, and remember too—
I will always be an Id bit better
Than you.

On Tides Of Passion
Or
The Lovers

She waits patiently, knowing her lover will always return to her. Theirs is not a hidden clandestine tryst—together they fling their love openly under blue skies, silver moons, in green velvet caverns or on coastal rocks.

Theirs is truly an endless love; she always races to embrace him, never questioning his absences, only welcoming wildly his return—

He hurries to her, strewing ahead of him glistening jewels encased in shell and sand crystal—his offerings cover his love. She watches as he comes toward her— closer and closer, "He's coming, he's coming." Boas of white froth frame her; she knows he is near.

They consummate their love, then locked in close embrace they roll about, flaunting their loving— making their own music, hearing only the songs of the seabirds above them. Sun can shine, rain can fall; it makes no difference to them.

Too soon the time comes for him to return whence he came, to renew himself again. He leaves, always roaring, "I'll be back."

One day I stood upon the beach, and as he went away, I thought I heard her say, "We have to stop meeting this way"—

This is the love story of the surf and the shore—

Nothing more—

(Shame on you.)

The Rejected Juror

Down, down ego!
Come now fallen pride!
The judge told you
     There is nothing personal involved.
Ah, but yes, still way down
       Deep, deep inside—
Why do you feel so dejected?
So pushed aside?
Is it because your peers are
     Going to a party and
       You are not invited?

Ode To A Cucumber

Little cucumber,
I've got your number.
So sweet and green
Scrubbed so clean,
I know you really like to drink a lot,
I can see you heading for that crock—

If only you hadn't crawled along the ground
You never would have found
        Yourself made into a pickle.
For one so sweet, you'll end up sour
Soaking in brine for many an hour.
You will lie in a jar so smelly
Somewhere
In some deli,
Till you are sold across the counter.
That will be your end—
        My little green friend—

(Your) City Property (Park)

Broken benches

Men, and fences

Littered pathways

Cluttered minds, winos
Nodding in the sun

Pigeon painted statues

No roller skating
No bike riding
No ball playing

This is your park—
Enjoy it—

The Relative Account

If you die and leave a will
Mourning relatives will fight until
It is broken, litigated unto death and still
    they'll mourn
Counting every nickel you had since you were born.

So spend my darlings while you may—
Enjoy bankbooks, C.D.'s or I.R.A.'s.
Let them say
You lived "December as though it were May."
You spent every last cent—
Darn it.

"They Are Not Sick,
 They Are Dying, A Most Natural Thing To Do."

Father Tom
Almost always catches their last act,
In fact
He is usually master of ceremonies at the event.
It's just the old familiar change of
Life to death
To
Life eternal.